I Wish Francisco Franco Would Love Me

Gloria Mindock

Nixes Mate Books
Allston, Massachusetts

Copyright © 2018 Gloria Mindock

Book design by d'Entremont
Cover photograph from the collection of Lauren Leja

All rights reserved. This book or any portion thereof may not be reproduced or used in any manner whatsoever without the express written permission of the publisher except for the use of brief quotations in a book review or scholarly journal.

ISBN 978-0-9993971-9-0

Nixes Mate Books
POBox 1179
Allston, MA 02134
nixesmate.pub/books

For Catherine Sasanov
For Andrey Gritsman

Contents

I

Love	3
Nenuca, a nickname for Carmen	4
Give Franco a gun so he can shoot me or give it to the *Moroccan* units to do.	5
Filling	6
Engulf	7
Coldness	8
And	9
Lost	10
Me	11
Valley of the Fallen	12
Calling	13
Carmen Polo, Lady Necklaces, 2017	14

II

Dictator	17
Clouds	18
The Hunger Years	19
Reaching	20
Les Milles	22
Credo Legionardo	23
Home	24
Hugging	25
Orbit	26

III

Blue Fascist Shirt	28
Houses	29
Disappearance in Another Country	31
The Visit	32
Mascots	33
Flames	34
The Gesture	35
Embrace	36
Without Peace	37

IV

The Man	39
Outspoken	40
The Spiral	42
Dirty Looks Seeps on the Sidewalk	43
A Story of Murder	44
Bye-Bye Franco	45
Splattered	46
The Fruit Fly	47
Waiting	49

I Wish Francisco Franco Would Love Me

Wall

Gravity is dangerous.
I'm stuck, can't float...
Abandoned by the stars.

When one falls, someone dies of neglect.

Today, I do my usual –
go to work, come home, write...
All these things engulf me.

I'm worn out between walls.
When is it time to sleep?
Explode into dreams?

Waking up, I drink my coffee and
wait for a burst into precision.
Outside, I wish for flight,
pecking at some tree trunk like
a bird, laying on the clouds

drifting.

I

Love

Franco is aiming at my
reproductive system.
Apparently, he is a specialist
when it comes to love.

The parliament watches and hails
their approval.
The countries reaction appears
on the front page of the newspaper.

I gain strength.
Franco is decorated.
Another medal equipped and bolstered
hydroplaning my opposition.

An advance is made.
Conflict ahead.
A total war, complex and for
14 days, our love is eclipsed.

Nenuca, a nickname for Carmen

Hail Francisco Franco!
Fame has arrived.
Your son knows no better but to love you.
The wife does know better.
Still they both fade into the background.
A blurry assignment for them.

A library only celebrated by brutality.
Oh Nenuca, just love me and shut up.

Give Franco a gun so he can shoot me or give it to the *Moroccan* units to do.

Franco, pleased, fell in love when he
first saw me.
A courtship took place on evening walks.
Franco squeezed my hands too many times.
Clumsy man wearing me out!
This love is tedious.
The same thing every night.

For the sake of appearances,
I smile.

Filling

I reached for your hands.
They weren't there.
Eyes of water, lake filling –
I can't even float.

Sinking deep, my body is drowning.
Life now, only one sided.
Put on a life-jacket next time
to keep from swallowing the drops that
flow into my mouth.

No breathing.
Alone, waiting…
The pier calls.

Engulf

Vulgar little man with a torn retina
lunging for a woman.
You press against her at a meeting
thinking she would like it.
Are you really that grand?
Are you really a turbine engine?
Voom! Voom! Voom!

Franco, you are international.
Your name is known.
Telephone all the cats in the world and meow.

You open the wine and scream seven words.
Severing any connection to those around you.
Franco, you are a General now –
a raccoon holding a growl on your face,
teeth showing that you will bite.

Bodies fall quickly and bullets melt
into a big metal sheet.
You put on roller skates and twirl into dictatorship.

Coldness

Franco, you are too harsh to love.
A tyrant with a filth attached to your heart…decay.
They say you loved your family,
an achievement.

I am standing on a corner in Madrid looking
at your statue.
A coldness reflecting on the sidewalk.
The blood still reveals itself.
A Shadow showing no affection
for the bodies of the dead.

And

Despair claws into me.
Bitter destiny.
Fate is content and I cannot change this.
Everyone is getting murdered.
My breathe is gone.
The patterns of air changed.
Hints of dreary hours are arriving
and your impulse is kill.
Franco, what reasons possess you?
If I look at you too closely, I might see clearly.
Right now, my gaze speaks with the people.
With hearts bright, they stand… die.
Do you like all the flowers?
Franco, I am stretched out on the dirt.

Lost

My mind is crushed, flattened, bruised, banished…
into all the agonies of the world

It is true
I think about all the
inches of rain…
Sorrow does visit sometimes

Now that I am empty,
my dreams exaggerate peace,
where everyone pulls the sky into their eyes
wishing to hear
all the lost mourning

Me

I'm a precious menace, twisted.
Around my neck a necklace of blood
dripping down my dress.
Oddly, I like it.

My body eroding weirdly
not to mention my bones.
Brittle and awakened, poking
out of my skin.

This is a narrow road walked on,
on a big spinning globe.
Witness the transitions gone, beyond repair.
Creation, creation ending.
Language spoken, unspoken.
Irreplaceable.

Boundaries.
What matters for me is the cinders
left from flame, broken hearts and brains
trying to speak but can't.

Oh, it is pointless in this life.

Valley of the Fallen

I want to be covered in a net of names,
with yours.
Violent soil.
Mountain grass facing me because the
oblivion drove me to distort my sobs,
my barfing, the genocide, I am part of.
My body, architecture on display in the
Valley of the Fallen.

Self, I ran toward the smile of death.

Hours of bells, ringing
but quiet.

Calling

Sometimes the angels speak to me.
Usually around 11:00 PM. My name called.
Veil covering my heart? No, it's the blanket
keeping me warm.
The whiteness around the angel, fills my
temple blazing hot.
I'm on a threshold of something reflecting,
sounds quiet until I wish it would pass.

I saw a man slit his throat yesterday.
Later, his daughter jumped off the bridge.
All to avoid Franco's fascism
All to avoid him doing the slashing.

At 11:00 PM, my name is called.
It is not the angel this time.
It is three men holding guns.

The torture starts, terror...
Fear...
Oh Angel, why do you desert me now?
There are things you can never erase in life.
This is one of them.

Carmen Polo, Lady Necklaces, 2017

Franco would kill after watching a zarzuela
or really anything.
I imagine him shooting people to David Bowie's song,
"Let's Dance" as he danced around with a rifle
In his hand or to the gospel song,
"Swing Low Sweet Chariot."

The woman he loved was disgusted
when he was stern and brusk.
The notes from her mouth were screechy.
Her pearls bright around her neck.
She liked to censor everyone around her,
to protect her man.
Even she could not escape being trapped in marriage.
She always appeared with Franco.

Blood affected every household.
It was never red, always black, dark and
stormy.

She kept going back for a daily dose.
She could not help it.
Fancy dresses and traveling. She never knew that
Franco was erasing her heart.

Her heart won't recuperate the turmoil of the end.
Carmen isolated herself years later.
Did not want to hear about politics or Franco.

Poor thing. Who cares?

She should have been buried in a Mass grave. Nameless.

II

Dictator

A dictator is not a spectator.
A spectator is not a dictator.
Why do you make everyone in Spain listen?

Some will betray you, rise-up.
You do not love!
You do not love!
Brutal Franco!
Brutal Franco!
You slob!
Messy in the heart. Kicking it out of your chest.

Even your heart knows you have secrets
cascading down into your pants.

Throats are slit today, bullets are fired, bombs dropped.
Plaza's preserved as killing fields.

Big man Franco leaves terror.
Too many Fathers are dead.
Never to hold their children again.
Killing in Bejar today…
Fascist!
Randomly killing what suits you.

Clouds

Give a signal when to break into a run.
Waiting, waiting…
Heart beating…
Mind in a cage…
Keys are needed in the hands of the innocent.

Feel the coldness in your hand. Oh,
it was a dream, lost –

You became a cloud disappearing just
for the sake of it.
Unfortunately, Franco liked fog at night.
During the day clouds could not remain.

Inbetween the clouds and fog, daylight cried
tears of water, trembling, stormy…
humming into his mouth.

The Hunger Years

Exile people in chronological order.
Escort their bold harsh faces into
the pavement.
Gather their questions into a book and
serenade them. LaLaLaLa
Make them eat lentils and sweet potatoes.
Reprise their life over and over as they eat.
Thank them, as you kill them.
And walk away knowing they were really screwed.

Reaching

Empty shoes on the road,
clothing left,
death hugged so many today.

Others now will wear the shoes,
feel the garments against their skin
in this poor village.

Dead bodies, just another number of
statistics in this country.
Sad to be a disappearing shadow.

The world has adjusted to death.
Pain diluted into the living.
They are numb, hollow…

Life's boney fingers reach out, but
have been disembodied.
There will be no justice for the dead.
The implication of just not dealing with it
extends from country to country but…

The families weep, remember their loved ones and their
concern for action, buried with a secret longing –
a silence that breaks glass and stabs the unbroken.

Les Milles

In the distance, gunfire.
A little girl, age 10, sat in the
middle of rubble.
Raped, she didn't understand the
death on her lips.

So much loss, pain, fear, hurt, and loneliness
 in the ashes.

Years later, by Mount Teide, she was plucked out of a
life of volcanoes, where she was no longer broken,
playing with other children without troubled air.

A man rescued her and gave her
help in an internment camp in Les Milles
When transported, the Angels sang,
the world rejoiced, and one more was saved.
One less surrounded by dark colored roses,
a chill in the air and scars left on the face.

Credo Legionardo

You will never abandon a comrade
on the field during battle.
Discipline Men! Discipline!

Big killer Franco –
Men want to shoot you in the back.
Turn your head towards them Franco.
Look them in the eye as they fire.

But they don't fire.

You say, *execute them* and walk away.

A grin on your face…
Customary.

Home

Franco murdered memories.
The dead converse with their screams
in this paradise mourning a life
that was all over the place.
Death is cold.
Wailing is labor.
Waiting for a sleep to call,
they pick up the phone to darkness.

Hugging

Uniforms blend
as the military down drinks
into their mouths
Quenching a thirst for dead bodies,
they aim their guns, the bullets land
painfully into the skin
Dreams do not respond
to the screams
A hat falls on the ground boldly
hugging the blood

Orbit

One bomb lunges
Chars the sunrise
Whispering graves now a museum
Scars left
Bones face the other planets
A planet showing what exile is

III

Blue Fascist Shirt

Javier will not wear the blue fascist shirt to school.
He will not sing the fascist anthem.
He will line up with the other children.
He will not march.
He will be silent.
He won't follow the rules.
He will not hate.
Javier will not wear the blue fascist shirt…
because they killed his father.

Houses

The fascists break into all the houses they can.
Daily, nightly, it does not matter when.
Grabbing me, my family…
Shoving us into a truck. So many of us packed in.

The others can hear them killing us.
One by one, guns fire, bombs are heard, so many
pistols, rifles…

Run people run!
Run to the mountains!
Run!
You will be caught.

Years later, excavation.
A blue tarp covering bodies…
a silence, tears.
Before the terror, a smile. After terror, bones,
a body changing. The dead in a ditch.

An image of hell coming back from the dead.
History told.
If an expression could be left,

it would express, please
do not step on us.
We've had enough.
Now that you found us, you cannot
sweep us back under the dirt.

Disappearance in Another Country

Investigate the voices buried beneath dirt,

all the white cars being driven around.

Disappearance: a villager seeing the
same face twice.

Bodies incinerated and dumped into
water. Hell dumped into the sea.

Ashes wash up. The tortures are vicious.

An evil for the lost,
all the white cars driving
look for a name, a body to own,
a purity to shove into a trunk...

The Visit

Dead bodies are sealed on your lips.
A kiss of blood.
The taste navigates you into blackness –
consuming…

Death meets you, seeps into your porous soul –
exhuming your hands to kill.
This is your foundation.
Death lodged inside of you.

Do you ever have nightmares?
Does any space open with light?
Evil continues, the people close their eyes,
try to erase the days for when they do not exist.

They call it the visit, limitless.

Mascots

Franco leaves bodies for mascots.
In each hand he holds a phone, talks at his desk.
There are feathers he gives to the teamsters of Slovakia.
They are so impressed by this gesture, they fail to
recognize they are being electrocuted.
How suave Franco is!

In the hallway, there are monks creeping
in the dust to get to the kitchen to cook madly.
It is floury in there and the liquid keeps running
from the bowl.

Flames

Bomb Guernica into a disappearing hell.
Destruction creating loss…
They jumped into a ditch on the
side of the road lying flat in utter fear.

Can't talk

Charred bodies

Sleep, you are about to vanish.
A showdown with an introduction to death.

The Gesture

Twenty-seven shot and dumped
in a mass grave.
Go away Franco!
To do this in the middle of the night or
at anytime is a wound spilling blood
into the eyes.

It is about time we see justice.
All those bodies have names.
Families cry missing loved ones.

There is no decent burial.

Good-bye is abortive.
For hours the wind blows…

Embrace

The rifle waits…
The pistol waits…
Bullets fire and embrace my body.

Blood seeps out looking for a new
shelter to hold it…
abandoning me.

A procession, a parade, the blood marches
in the grass.
Scared, not wanting to be alone, this is
beyond any words I can say, any tears
I can cry.

It is time to leave.
All I can think about is…
who I loved.

With eyes closed, the dream begins.
God listened.
My veins are roots that grab onto the intimate.

Without Peace

Witnessing the remains beneath, the dirt
is on you Francisco.
Fragments of life lost, blood of the innocent.

On this day, the survivors weep like they do every day.
Their skin is hollow from starvation, the bread they try
to eat is ashen.
No church bells ring today. No communion is taken.
No host of our Lord swallowed.
The only incense in the air is that of rotting bodies.
"Peace be with you" are the only words said.
Means nothing.

Christ on the cross cries. Hope is lost.
The prayers from lips drip down off bodies.
No mercy.
Under the skin, a stain.

There is a cross inside each body where
the suffering suffers with bullets.
Pinning them into eternity.
Finally giving them rest, a home untouched by evil.

IV

The Man

Pacifier, un-pacifier
Commander: successful, un-successful
Firepower, machine gun
Repelling, not repelling
Combat: casualties, no casualties
Nice day, not nice day
Bullets hit, bullets miss
Death, no death
Thank you, no thank you
Rage, no rage
Ambition: stable, not stable

Descend! Descend! Descend!

Widowed, not widowed

Oh Franco, *you know how to treat girls.*

Outspoken

Disappointed, Franco's life isn't going
like he wanted.
Some, are betraying him.
He is no ones fool.

In the newspaper, he wrote a
one page ad.
When the people saw it,
they were perplexed.
Outspoken Franco, carved the hearts
out of many by his rhetoric.

Franco opposes, opposes, opposes!
Collapsing his fingers around the pen tightly,
he is writing something again.
A dancing brain with visions!

All are terminal.
Say good-bye.
He is about to break your
body on concrete.

On beautiful people, grieve for your life.
A stagecoach with a princess will not take you away.

The absence of the villagers is seen only
by the survivors.
They cry.

In the stairwell, Franco laughs hysterically
like a hyena, running up and down the steps
colliding with himself.

The Spiral

Franco, why are you dismayed on this
cool Autumn day?
Why are the elite rejecting you?
After all, you keep climbing up
the social ladder.
Up and up you go.

You paint in water colors,
a beautiful life.
The colors fading into each other.
The blood in the grass is disappearing.
Revealing a blackened soil.

Down and down you go.

Dirty Looks Seeps on the Sidewalk

He is a mess,
a selfless solemn scrap.
Put him in a cage to protect all of us.
Do religious rites and rattle his dirty looks
into a book about a murderous fool.
A muscular weasel…
No one wants him.
He spits phlegm up and aims a rifle.
Leave and don't detain me.
I don't want you on my doorstep.

A Story of Murder

He was a man who wanted to
lay eggs like a hen.
He had abandonment issues, bad omens
surrounded his sight.
Giving birth to an egg for him was painful but
he did have brilliant feet!
After the eggs were on the ground, he licked
each and everyone, contemplating their names.
They were put in a leather box, the yolky little things!
He shook them as if they were hell burning
prematurely trapped into false landscapes.
Finally, a needle was stuck and he sucked them
up into his mouth and dreamt death.
Bye-bye little ones.
He always wanted an exit that was fatal.

Bye-Bye Franco

Bye-Bye Franco.
I am not saddened by bullets.
The danger you exposed me to…
Disappointing.
My feelings kept unknown.

Ready to perish,
I join the others.
The way you run your country,
Melodramatic!

Fat chance I will polish the
decorations on your jacket.

Command the Regulares!
Protect your units.
Talk, Talk, Talk!
Rules, Rules, Rules!

I break them.

Splattered

So you imbecile carrying no weapon
in your hands, what are you but hospitable
firing from a tank.
That is your gun killing minds in Spain
with liquid crying from heads.

The Fruit Fly

The fruit fly landed on Franco's nose and
would not move.
The skin was tasty.
The fly started eating and eating until
only bone was left.
Francisco could no longer smell the slaughter.
More fruit flies landed
on his skin and chowed
and chowded.
Bony man Franco disintegrating into
all the fruit flies mouths.
Spain was liberated!

Waiting

Waiting for an angel to circle, drop
threads on our faces, we cover our eyes
in this system of the obsolete.

After awhile, we are meek in our armchair
watching TV…
feeling lazy, thinking, we have time.

Gather yourself.
The bullets fly on this hot summer day
into your skin.

Acknowledgments

I would like to thank the following literary magazines where some of these poems were published:
Constellations: A Journal of Poetry and Fiction, *Ibbetson Street Magazine*, *Muddy River Poetry Review*, *Unlikely Stories*, *Bagel Bards Anthology*, and *Writing in a Woman's Voice*.

"Waiting" received the 5th Moon Prize from *Writing in a Woman's Voice*.

The poem "Gunfire" which appeared in *Muddy River Poetry Review* is now titled "Les Milles."

"Carmen Polo, Lady Necklaces, 2017," Back Story of a Poem, Chris Rice Cooper Blog

Thank you to Tim Suermondt, Pui Ying Wong, Nina Rubinstein Alonso, Doug Holder, Harris Gardner, Zvi A. Sesling, Jonathan Penton, Chris Rice Cooper, and Beate Sigriddaughter for their support of these poems.

Thank you to Michael McInnis, Annie Pluto, and Philip Borenstein of Nixes Mate for believing in my work and giving it a home.

Thank you to my Mom and Dad, Kellis, Richard, Alexander, and Bill.

Thank you to Dzvinia Orlowsky, Catherine Sasanov, Mary Bonina, Carol Schmidt, Janie Gregorich, Sandy Shipp, Shirley Prescott and to all the writers that attend The Poetry Roundtable. You all are the best!

About The Author

Gloria Mindock is the founding editor of Červená Barva Press and one of the USA editors for *Levure Litteraire* (France). She is the author of *Whiteness of Bone* (Glass Lyre Press, 2016), *La Porțile Raiului* (Ars Longa Press, Romania) translated into the Romanian by Flavia Cosma, *Nothing Divine Here*, *Blood Soaked Dresses*, and 3 chapbooks. Widely published in the USA and abroad, her poetry has been translated and published into the Romanian, Croatian, Serbian, Montenegrin, Spanish, Estonian, and French. Gloria was awarded the Ibbetson Street Press Lifetime Achievement Award, and was the recipient of the Allen Ginsberg Award for Community Service by the Newton Writing and Publishing Center. Gloria recently was published in *Gargoyle*, *Constellations: A Journal of Poetry and Fiction*, *Muddy River Poetry Review*, *Unlikely Stories*, and *Nixes Mate Review* and anthology. She is currently the Poet Laureate in Somerville, Massachusetts.

42° 19' 47.9" N   70° 56' 43.9" W

Nixes Mate is a navigational hazard in Boston Harbor used during the colonial period to gibbet and hang pirates and mutineers.

Nixes Mate Books features small-batch artisanal literature, created by writers who use all 26 letters of the alphabet and then some, honing their craft the time-honored way: one line at a time.

nixesmate.pub/books

www.ingramcontent.com/pod-product-compliance
Lightning Source LLC
Chambersburg PA
CBHW070440010526
44118CB00014B/2130